NATURAL WONDERS AND DISASTERS

NATURAL
WONDERS
AND DISASTERS

BILLY GOODMAN

Little, Brown and Company
Boston   Toronto   London

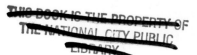

First Edition

ISBN 0-316-32016-1

Library of Congress Cataloging-in-Publication Data

Goodman, Billy.
    Natural wonders and disasters / Billy Goodman.
        p.   cm.   (A Planet Earth book)
    Summary: Introduces the world of geology by explaining why natural disasters and wonders happen.
    ISBN 0-316-32016-1
    1. Geology Juvenile literature. 2. Landforms Juvenile literature. 3. Natural disasters Juvenile literature. 4. Earth Juvenile literature. [1. Natural disasters. 2. Geology.]
    I. Title. II. Series.
    QE29.G66 1991
    550   dc20   90-53706

A TERN ENTERPRISE BOOK

10 9 8 7 6 5 4 3 2 1

Natural Wonders and Disasters
was prepared and produced by
Tern Enterprise, Inc.
15 West 26th Street
New York, NY 10010

Editor: Stephen Williams
Designer: Judy Morgan
Photography Editor: Ede Rothaus

Additional Photography Credits:
6–7 © David Noble/FPG International; 16–17 © Dave G. Houser;
24–25 © Rory Lysaght/Gamma Liaison; 44–45 © Rick Doyle;
64–65 © T. Algire/FPG International; 74–75 © Rick Doyle

Typeset by The Interface Group
Color separations by Excel Graphic Arts Co.
Printed and bound in Hong Kong by LeeFung-Asco Printers Ltd.

Dedication

To my parents, Doris K. Goodman and
Theodore J. Goodman.

Acknowledgements

Barbara Goldburg made many helpful suggestions
on the manuscript on short order, for which I am
grateful. And thanks to Dorothy Tao, Information
Specialist with the National Center for Earthquake
Engineering Research in Buffalo, New York, for
pointing out many useful resources.

For taking time to discuss their specialties and to
answer questions, I'd like to thank the following scientists: Lucy Jones, William Kaula, Miles Lawrence,
Allan Lindh, Jason Morgan, and Carl Turkstra.

CONT

E N T S

INTRODUCTION

The earth sometimes seems very alive. That's puzzling, considering that it's made of just rocks and dirt and oceans, surrounded by air.

But these parts of our planet are in constant motion and change. Every once in a while, they remind us just how powerful the earth is. An earthquake changes the course of a stream. A volcano blows its top, possibly affecting the world's weather for months. Days of rain send a swollen river over its banks, flooding a valley. A hurricane gains strength over the ocean, and comes to the coast to blast a community with destructive wind and water.

Such events are called *natural disasters* because they usually cause incredible damage to people and their belongings. They are examples of what can happen when the normally slow-moving parts of the earth move wildly or when the air and

water of the earth conspire to create a storm.

Interestingly, the same forces of the earth that sometimes cause disasters are also responsible for many spectacular natural wonders, such as five-mile-high mountains and six-mile-deep ocean trenches, the Grand Canyon, and Old Faithful. When the earth shifts violently, an earthquake might be the result. But when it moves more slowly, it might make a mountain.

The structure of the earth provides some clues to its occasionally violent behavior. The planet is not made of solid rock all the way to the center, but rather has layers, like an avocado. The outer layer is called the *crust* and is thin like the skin of the avocado. The next layer, the "flesh" of our earthly avocado, is the *mantle*. It is made of denser, hotter rock than the crust. Finally, at the center of the earth, like the pit of an avocado, is the *core*. The total distance from the center of the earth to the surface is nearly 4,000 miles. No one has ever drilled a hole as deep as the core, but scientists believe that temperatures here are extremely hot—so hot in fact that the outer part of the iron and nickel core is thought to be liquid. The inner core, compressed under the weight of the entire earth, is solid.

INTRODUCTION   11

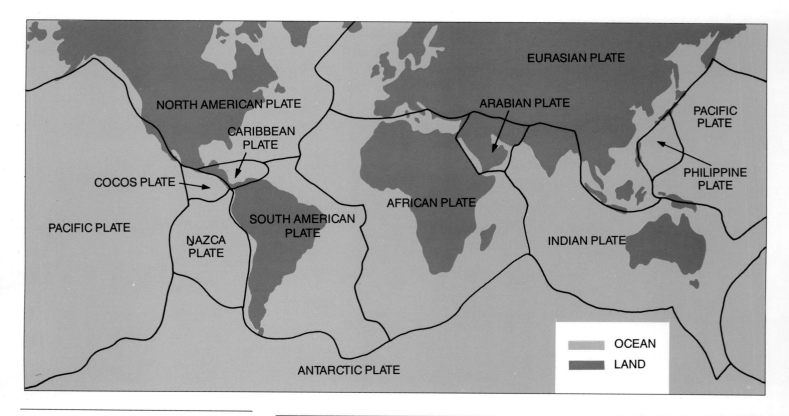

NORTH AMERICAN PLATE

EURASIAN PLATE

CARIBBEAN PLATE

ARABIAN PLATE

PACIFIC PLATE

COCOS PLATE

AFRICAN PLATE

PHILIPPINE PLATE

PACIFIC PLATE

NAZCA PLATE

SOUTH AMERICAN PLATE

INDIAN PLATE

ANTARCTIC PLATE

OCEAN
LAND

The earth's crust, or top layer, is broken into many plates, as this map shows. Where they meet, plates can dive beneath another, slide past each other, or collide head on and crumple up. Earthquakes and volcanoes usually occur near plate boundaries. These folded hills (right) near Palm Springs, California, are on the San Andreas Fault. West of the fault, a slice of California is moving toward the northwest. It moves at about the same rate that fingernails grow.

The Earth as a Jigsaw Puzzle

- The Mediterranean Sea is being squeezed shut.
- The Atlantic Ocean is becoming wider.
- The Himalaya Mountains are growing.
- The Appalachians are getting shorter.

These bizarre notions are not science fiction; they are scientific fact. Scientists explain them with a theory about how the earth is built, called *plate tectonics* (the Greek word *tektonicos* refers to *builder*).

Simply put, this theory says that the earth's surface is divided up into a number of plates that fit together like pieces of a jigsaw puzzle. In all, there are about 10 large plates and a number of smaller ones. Each plate is made up of the crust plus the top layer of the mantle—together, they are about 100 miles thick. The plates ride around on the mantle almost like rafts on a lake.

Some plates are entirely ocean floor, such as the Cocos plate off of Mexico, but others cover ocean floor and continents. For example, the large North American plate contains the continent of North America and the western half of the floor of the Atlantic Ocean. Continents are made of thick, but light, crust. Ocean floor is thinner, heavier crust.

Plates are constantly moving, at speeds of up to several inches a year. They are pushed by hot rock the consistency of molasses—called *magma*—that squeezes its way to the surface from the center of the earth.

Plates meet each other at cracks in the earth called *faults* (faults can also occur elsewhere). Three things can happen where plates meet:

- The edges of the plates can slide past each other in opposite directions. This is known as a *transform fault* or a *strike-slip fault*. Earthquakes are common along this sort of boundary.

- The edges of the plates can pull apart from each other. Hot magma rises from inside the earth to "heal" the crack. Such boundaries are usually underwater. In places where they are on land—such as Iceland and East Africa—volcanoes are common.

- The edges of the plates can crash into each other. Mountains, volcanoes, and deep ocean trenches result from these collisions.

© Greg Vaughn

Red-hot lava forms a "curtain of fire" during the Puu O eruption of Hawaii's Kilauea Volcano. Many homes were destroyed during this 1986 eruption. Kilauea itself has been erupting almost constantly since 1983.

People and Natural Disasters

An earthquake in an uninhabited region would hardly be a disaster. But an earthquake that flattened homes or injured people would be considered a disaster.

The people that natural disasters harm most are those from the poor countries that make up the Third World. Third World cities are often more crowded than other cities, making the effects of a natural disaster worse. The homes people live in are sometimes poorly made, from the standpoint of standing up to the violent shaking of an earthquake or the 100-mile-per-hour winds of a tropical cyclone. When a disaster does strike, the government may not have enough money to help the people quickly and effectively. And, sadly, sometimes people must ignore the risks of natural disasters so that they can make enough money to feed their families. For example, often the best farmland is next to a river that floods periodically, because when a river floods, it brings nutrients to the land which help crops grow. So, following a flood that may have destroyed many homes and killed many people, survivors return to the floodplain to begin farming again. People, rich and poor, have a knack for saying, "It won't happen to me."

In the 1930s, lack of rainfall combined with overuse of the land in the Great Plains resulted in a natural disaster known as the Dust Bowl. Good soil dried up and blew away.

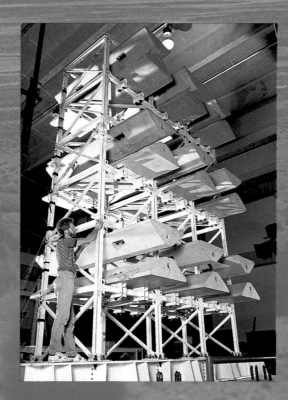

EARTH

We are almost never aware of the motion of the plates of the earth. But, if we had millions of years to watch, we could see the results of that motion, as some continents moved apart, others moved closer, and still others were torn in two.

Sometimes, however, parts of the plates move suddenly. Having been stuck together for years, the edges of two plates may all of a sudden jump past one another. This violent motion is called an earthquake.

The motion may be at a fault between two plates. Or it may be at a fault within one plate where stress has caused a crack. The motion usually starts at a portion of the fault that is underground, called the *focus*. The point on the earth's surface directly above the focus is called the *epicenter*.

EARTHQUAKES

When a stuck section of a fault ruptures, the energy released travels through the earth in the form of waves. The waves radiate out from the focus, much like the waves on a pond when you throw a rock in the water. An earthquake produces several kinds of waves. All of them can be measured by an instrument called a seismograph, which records the vibrations of the earthquake. To describe the amount of energy released by an earthquake, seismologists (earthquake scientists) use the Richter scale. Named after Charles Richter, the man who designed it, the scale is based on the size of the vibrations charted on the seismograph.

The fastest is called the P or primary wave and is a kind of sound wave. Next comes the S or secondary wave. Another kind of wave radiates out from the epicenter and is called the surface wave.

More than one million earthquakes strike the globe each year, but most are too small for a person to feel. Superquakes—Richter magnitude 8 or above—occur, on average, only once or twice a decade. A magnitude 8 earthquake packs 10 times the punch of a magnitude 7 quake.

Even tiny quakes can be detected by seismographs. In fact some seismographs are too sensitive to be used on earth, where a truck rumbling miles away sends the needle jumping. So, instead, scientists use them on the moon where they can detect the waves generated by a meteorite as small as two pounds when it strikes anywhere on the moon.

Another way to describe an earthquake is its intensity, or degree of ground shaking. Intensity is not measured with an instrument, but is reported by trained observers. Two observers in the same place might describe an earthquake slightly differently. And an observer close to an earthquake's epicenter would feel greater intensity than someone farther away. One of the most used intensity scales is called the Modified Mercalli scale.

Portrait of the San Andreas

The photograph on the previous page shows what is left of a village in Iran after an earthquake in 1989. The great San Francisco earthquake of 1906 (above) was one of the strongest ever in the United States, and was estimated at 8.3 on the Richter Scale. The rumbling lasted 75 seconds; the fires started as a result of the quake lasted three days. In all, more than 700 people were killed.

In the soft light of dawn on April 18, 1906, a San Francisco police sergeant was making his rounds when he heard "a deep rumbling," according to Jay Robert Nash, author of *Darkest Hours*. Then, as he looked up the street, he saw an awful sight: "The whole street was undulating. It was as if the waves of the ocean were coming toward me." The great San Francisco Earthquake of 1906 had struck.

Another witness to the quake was a professor, Alexander McAdie. The quake woke McAdie up and he noted the time, 5:12 a.m., and after the first shock passed, calmly wrote, "Severe shaking lasting forty seconds." After a 10-second timeout, a second tremor lasted 25 seconds.

The quake, since estimated to

have been 8.3 on the Richter scale, destroyed much of San Francisco, which then had a population of about four hundred thousand. Thousands of buildings were damaged or even toppled by the shaking. Gas mains ruptured, setting off fires. But there wasn't much water to fight the flames, because the water mains also broke. So the huge fire raged unchecked for three days, destroying 520 city blocks and more than twenty-eight thousand buildings. Seven hundred people were killed.

The cause of the quake was a rupture along the most famous fault in North America, the San Andreas. The fault marks where two plates meet, the Pacific and the North American. The Pacific is now moving northwest at the average rate of about 2 inches a year (that's the speed your fingernails grow) and has been moving, at various very slow speeds, for hundreds of thousands of years. The edges of the plates occasionally become stuck. The rest of the plate continues to move and so stress builds up at the locked portion of the fault. Eventually, the stress gets so great that the fault breaks and the locked portion of the plate jumps to catch up.

The Pretty Big One

The 1906 quake was certainly a "big one." Smaller earthquakes have ruptured other parts of the San Andreas fault since that time. But the portion near San Francisco has not ruptured since 1906. When it does, geologists expect a large quake, which is why San Franciscans are said to be "waiting for the big one."

Some people thought it had come on October 17, 1989. The Bay Area was the focus of much of the nation's attention that day. The

third game of the baseball World Series, between the San Francisco Giants and the Oakland Athletics, was about to get underway at San Francisco's Candlestick Park. As A's shortstop Walt Weiss remembered it, he was jogging in the outfield when he stumbled. "I thought I hit a hole in the ground," he told the Oakland Tribune. "I was going to start checking the grass, but everything else started moving too. Then I knew it was an earthquake."

That earthquake has since become known as the Loma Prieta quake, named for the mountain near its epicenter about 60 miles south of downtown San Francisco. It measured 7.1 on the Richter scale. Many call it the "pretty big one."

In October, 1989, part of the San Andreas fault ruptured, causing what became known as the Loma Prieta earthquake. In parts of San Francisco buildings collapsed into the sidewalk even as neighboring buildings were undamaged (left). The shaking caused a 50-foot section of the Bay Bridge to collapse (below).

Two earthquakes rocked Mexico City on two consecutive days in September, 1985. The epicenter of the quakes was more than 200 miles away, where one of the earth's plates dives below the Mexican coast. The first quake lasted two minutes and left 4,000 dead and 10,000 wounded. In all, 400 buildings crumbled and 700 more were severely damaged.

Mayhem in Mexico

Thursday morning, September 19, 1985 began as an ordinary morning in Mexico City, the western hemisphere's largest city, with over 18 million people. At 7:18 the rush hour was just beginning. Children were walking to school, or waiting on street corners for buses.

Two hundred and thirty miles away in the Pacific Ocean, a piece of the Cocos plate picked that moment to tear and slide beneath the Mexi-

can coast into the Middle America trench. Oceanic crust always dives beneath continental crust when the two collide, since oceanic crust is heavier. The process is called *subduction*.

The first seismic waves from that subduction took more than a minute to reach Mexico City. When they did, tremors measuring 8.1 on the Richter scale lasted more than two minutes and devastated the center of the city. Four hundred buildings crumbled to the ground; seven hundred more were badly damaged. Included in the tally were two hundred schools. The country's major television network went off the air. Telephone service was disrupted and electricity was cut to large areas of the city.

The destruction was just beginning. The following day, a second earthquake, measuring 7.3 on the Richter scale, toppled some of the buildings the first one merely damaged.

Agony in Armenia

The Soviet Republic of Armenia is a mountainous region east of Turkey. It is a seismically active region where the large African plate drives northward to meet the Eurasian plate, and several small plates also push and shove. The resulting compression is responsible for the Alps and mountains across Turkey and the Near East, and has touched off many devastating earthquakes from Italy to Pakistan.

On December 7, 1988, one of those devastating quakes leveled all or parts of several Armenian cities, killing an estimated fifty thousand people, leaving more than one-half million homeless, and causing Soviet President Mikhail Gorbachev to cut short a trip to the United States.

The death toll was higher than a quake measuring 6.9 on the Richter scale would produce in California. The reason is that the houses and apartment buildings in Armenia weren't built to stand up to an earthquake. Dr. Roger Bilham of the University of Colorado told The New York Times: "It is buildings, not earthquakes" that kill people. Many of the buildings were made of low-quality concrete, without steel to strengthen them.

The earthquake that hit Soviet Armenia in December, 1988, was not especially strong, measuring 6.9 on the Richter scale. But many buildings collapsed because they were made of concrete without steel rods to strengthen it. Such so-called unreinforced masonry is very dangerous in an earthquake. Thus, the saying, "buildings, not earthquakes, kill people."

© Vlastimir Shone/Gamma Liaison

Buildings That Stand Up to Quakes

Just as in 1906, fires caused a lot of damage to San Francisco in the Loma Prieta earthquake of 1989 (previous page). Because steel bends before it breaks, buildings made with lots of steel tend to stand up well to earthquakes. Buildings made mostly of concrete, such as this building in Mexico City, are prone to collapse.

The last place most people would want to be during an earthquake is high up in a skyscraper, where even the motion on windy days can be enough to make some people ill. But, in fact, modern high-rises make good refuges during an earthquake. "They are designed to withstand strong winds," says civil engineer Carl Turkstra, "and so are not particularly vulnerable to earthquakes."

Falling debris causes most injuries and deaths during an earthquake. Often, homes in poor countries are made of mud, bricks, or stone. These heavy materials may not be well joined, and the walls may collapse during heavy shaking, bringing down the roof. Some cities don't allow buildings to have parapets because these and other

unsupported structures may topple during a quake.

Older buildings of unreinforced masonry—that is, bricks and concrete—are much more dangerous than modern buildings that have plenty of steel in them. The reason is simple: Steel bends before it breaks, while masonry breaks suddenly. A paper clip demonstrates steel's advantages. Bend it a little and it snaps back. Bend it a little more and it remains bent, but unbroken. Breaking a paper clip requires forceful bending, perhaps back and forth.

In the Mexico City quake, some steel buildings were too damaged to repair and so were torn down. But at least they absorbed the energy of the earthquake without collapsing.

Hard Rock or Bowl of Jell-O

If you hit one side of a large boulder with a hammer, a friend touching the boulder on the other side might barely feel the vibrations. But tap one edge of a bowl of Jell-O and the whole mass will start quivering. So, given the choice, do you build a city on bedrock, or on a bowl of Jell-O?

Mexico City, unfortunately, is built on a bowl of Jell-O, otherwise known as the bed of an ancient lake. The soft clay beneath the buildings amplifies the shaking when earthquake waves pass. The result: Many buildings that might have withstood the 1985 earthquake if they had been built on bedrock were shaken off their foundation.

Soft soil also played a role in the damage caused by the Loma Prieta earthquake. Much of San Francisco's Marina district is built on landfill—loose material dumped into shallow water to create new land. When this sandy, waterlogged soil is set vibrating by an earthquake, the individual grains of sand become stirred up with the water. The soil behaves more like a liquid than a solid, and is unable to support anything built on it. Therefore the building collapses.

Courtesy National Center for Earthquake Engineering Research/State University of New York at Buffalo

Scientists trying to protect buildings during earthquakes use this "shake table" and a model of a six-story tall building to simulate the effects of an earthquake. From these experiments, scientists develop safer building techniques.

Ground motion caused by an earthquake is measured using an instrument called a seismograph. These tracings (right) record an earthquake that hit Quebec, Canada, in 1988. The tracings were made 125 miles from the earthquake, in Maine. Sometimes animals behave strangely before an earthquake (opposite page). They may run wildly, bark in fear, and come out of underground burrows. No one is sure why this happens. The animals certainly don't "know" that an earthquake is about to happen. But they may sense a change in their environment, such as gasses released from inside the earth prior to an earthquake.

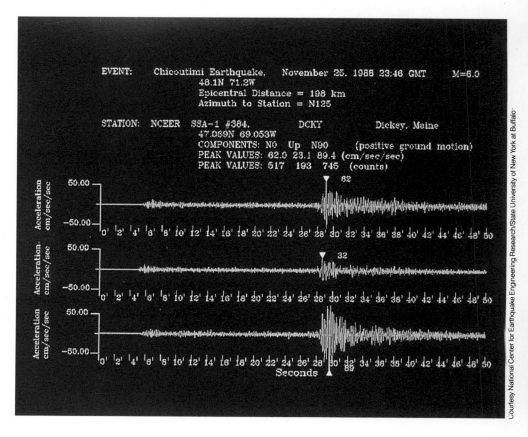

Can Earthquakes Be Predicted?

When asked if scientists could predict earthquakes, Lucy Jones, a seismologist with the United States Geological Survey (USGS), in Pasadena, California, replied, "We can't." She went on to say that she doesn't think scientists will "ever be able to say there'll be an earthquake tomorrow at three o'clock." Absolute certainty just isn't part of science, according to Dr. Jones

Nevertheless, seismologists can and do make long-term earthquake forecasts. For example, one year before the Loma Prieta quake, a panel of geologists issued forecasts for several parts of the San Andreas fault. For the part that eventually ruptured at Loma Prieta, they predicted that over the next thirty years there was a thirty percent chance of an earthquake of magnitude 6.5. They based that forecast on how often earthquakes had occured at that segment in the past and on the movement of that segment relative to other segments.

Occasionally, seismologists issue warnings of an increased possibility of an earthquake for the next three days. These are based on a simple observation: About one in seventeen earthquakes is followed by a larger quake. So, if a magnitude 5 quake strikes an area, there's a one in seventeen chance of a larger quake hitting the same area within three days or so. That's enough of a chance that geologists might issue a warning. An earthquake that occurs immediately before another one is called a *foreshock*. Unfortunately, foreshocks are often as dangerous as earthquakes.

Can Animals Predict Earthquakes?

Plenty of folk tales and even a little scientific research suggest that animals sometimes act oddly before an earthquake. There are stories of birds leaving an area, of dogs barking wildly, of cattle running off, of mice acting dazed, even of fish leaping out of the water.

In 1975, Chinese authorities used reports of animals behaving oddly to help them predict an earthquake. In early January they issued a warning for the next six months. Then in early February they gave a twenty-four-hour warning and evacuated townspeople to the countryside. An earthquake measuring 7.3 struck on February 4, causing great destruction but few deaths. Apparently, reports of strange animal behavior increased in the days preceding the quake, as did reports of changes in well-water quality. But according to Dr. Jones of the USGS, who spent a year doing research in China, it was really an incredible five hundred

WORST EARTHQUAKES OF THIS CENTURY

YEAR	COUNTRY	DEAD	RICHTER SCALE
1976	China	200,000*	7.8
1927	China	200,000	8.3
1923	Japan	100,000	8.3
1920	China	100,000	8.6
1908	Italy	83,000	7.5
1970	Peru	66,794	7.7
1990	Iran	40,000	7.7
1939	Turkey	30,000	7.9
1935	India	30,000	7.5
1939	Chile	28,000	8.3

*According to the official Chinese government estimates. Other estimates have ranged as high as 800,000 dead.

foreshocks that hit the area over twelve hours that prompted the Chinese to begin the evacuation.

Nevertheless, Dr. Jones is especially intrigued by the Chinese reports of snakes leaving their winter burrows just before the earthquake, only to freeze to death. Unfortunately, using animals to help predict earthquakes has a long way to go before it's reliable. Two years after the successful prediction, an earthquake struck with no warning and killed 240,000 people.

MOUNTAINS

The forces that unleash earthquakes are the same ones that build mountains. When a continent on one plate collides with a continent on another plate, the crust at the front of both plates is squeezed into the air. The collision may continue for millions of years, all the while pushing up the mountains.

The leading edges of continents or plates, which are the first to make contact in a collision, are often underwater. So, as the plates squeeze together, the bottom of the ocean is pushed high into the air. That's why geologists often find fossils of ancient sea creatures in high mountains.

There are some kinds of mountains that aren't formed directly by the movements of plates. An example is the Grand Teton range of western Wyoming, a string of mountains roughly 40 miles long by 15 miles wide. The Tetons are spectacular, rising up like a wall at the western side of a broad, flat valley called Jackson Hole.

The Tetons and Jackson Hole are the result of movement along a fault that forms the boundary between them. On the west side of the fault, a block of the earth's crust thrust upward, making the mountain range. Meanwhile, east of the fault, another block fell, making Jackson Hole. The movement continues; the Tetons are very young in geological time—about 10 million years—and still growing.

Mt. Everest, at 29,028 feet above sea level, is the world's tallest mountain. It is located in Nepal.

Himalayas

Tibetans call it *Chomolungma*, which means "Goddess Mother of the Land." We know it as Mt. Everest, the tallest mountain of the tallest group of mountains in the world, the Himalayas. Everest stands 29,028 feet above sea level. For 1,500 miles, the curve of the Himalayas is like a shield separating India from the Tibetan plateau of China. Thirty Himalayan peaks soar past twenty-four thousand feet.

The Himalayas are young mountains and they look it—sharp, jagged peaks are a sign that erosion hasn't yet had much impact. In geological time, it wasn't too long ago that the Indo-Australian plate plowed into the Eurasian plate using what is now India as a battering ram. Part of the Indian plate has been scraped off and shoved on top of the Eurasian plate.

The collision began about twenty-five million years ago and continues to this day. The Himalayas are actually growing, perhaps a foot or so a century.

Mt. Nuptse is only the 19th tallest peak in the Himalayan range. But at a height of 25,726 feet, it is taller than all other mountains outside the continent of Asia.

The Andes

While not as high as the Himalayas, the Andes are still impressive. The various ranges of the Andes run the entire length of the continent of South America—5,500 miles. Among the mountains is the highest peak in the Western Hemisphere, the 22,831-foot Mt. Aconcagua, in Argentina. Forty seven other Andean peaks rise above twenty thousand feet.

Like the Himalayas, the Andes formed as the result of the collision of two plates, but in a way quite different from the Himalayas. Instead of continent crashing into continent, the Andes are the result of the sea floor plunging beneath the continent. As the Nazca plate dives, it pulls the front edge of the continent down with it, forming a deep ocean trench. The sinking plate melts and the magma rises to the surface, supplying at least 20 active volcanoes.

Cuernos del Paine, in the Torres del Paine national park, Chile. This mountain is typical of the dramatic peaks of the Andes mountains of South America.

EARTH 33

Old Mountains

Old mountains are gentle mountains. Erosion by wind and water softens their jagged peaks and gradually reduces their height. The Appalachian Mountains of the eastern United States make up one of the oldest ranges in the world. Geologists say they began forming about four hundred million years ago, and thus are nearly one-tenth the age of the earth.

Before resting where they are now, the landmasses that were to become North America and Europe were separated by an ancient ocean. Beginning about four hundred million years ago those land masses collided and pushed up the ancient Appalachians. A short while later, a land mass that is present day Siberia collided with Europe on its eastern edge to form the Ural Mountains.

Beginning about two-hundred million years ago, the North American and European plates reversed themselves and began to pull away. It's been all downhill for the Appalachian Mountains since.

The Appalachian Mountains of the

eastern United States are one of the

oldest mountain ranges in the world.

The Green Mountains of Vermont,

part of the Appalachians, show their

age by their gently balding peaks.

VOLCANOES

Volcanoes are mountains that may be built, or destroyed, while you watch. In 1943, as a Mexican farmer worked in his cornfield, a red-hot rock shot out of a hole in the ground. The farmer tried to bandage the earth's wound by filling it with dirt, but when he looked the next day the hole had become a cone, six feet in diameter and twenty inches high, with a crater in the middle. In a year, the volcano, Paricutin, was twelve-hundred-feet high and a half-mile wide at the base. You can bet that the farmer moved his field.

There are more than 1,300 volcanoes in the world, although only about 600 can be classified as active. The others are either dormant (quiet for centuries, though they could become active again) or dead (not expected to erupt again). About 50 eruptions occur worldwide each year.

Geologists are working hard to better understand why volcanoes erupt, so they can warn people in advance. Often earthquakes precede an eruption, but because the quakes may come months before the blast, or only hours before, they are hard to use for precise forecasts.

Researchers predicted in 1978 that Mt. St. Helens in southwestern Washington was likely to erupt, "perhaps before the end of this century." They were right, of course, as Mt. St. Helens blew explosively on May 18, 1980, killing 57 people. Swarms of small earthquakes were detected at the mountain in the two months leading to the eruption. Although scientists couldn't predict the exact moment of eruption, they knew enough to keep people away. Their warnings kept many people from being killed.

Mt. Vesuvius, overlooking the sea at Naples, Italy, erupted in 79 A.D. and buried the city of Pompeii in mud and ash. Much has been learned about ancient Italian life from the well-preserved remains of the city.

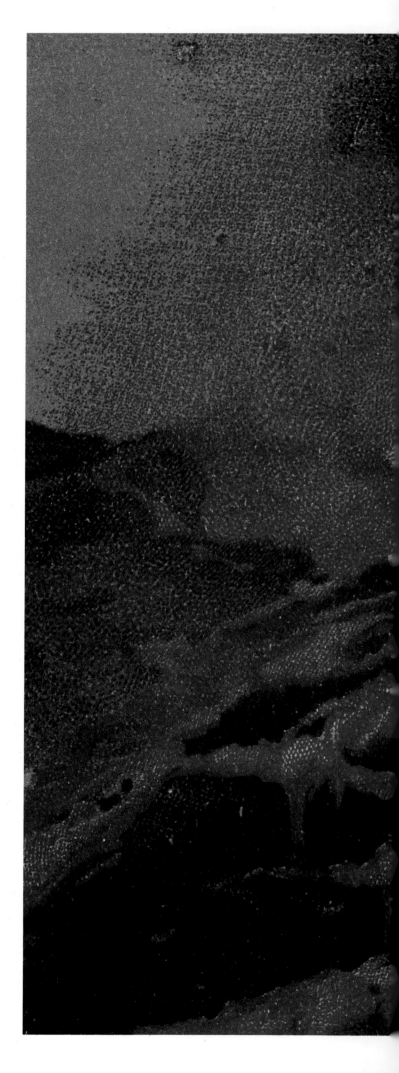

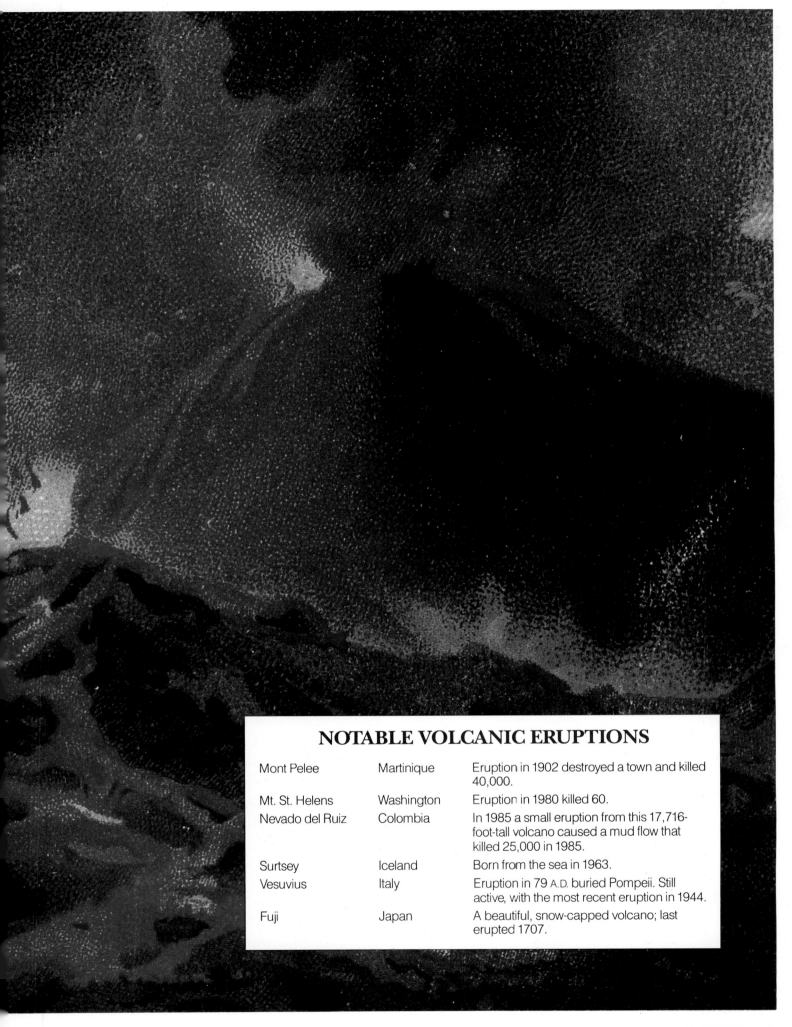

NOTABLE VOLCANIC ERUPTIONS

Mont Pelee	Martinique	Eruption in 1902 destroyed a town and killed 40,000.
Mt. St. Helens	Washington	Eruption in 1980 killed 60.
Nevado del Ruiz	Colombia	In 1985 a small eruption from this 17,716-foot-tall volcano caused a mud flow that killed 25,000 in 1985.
Surtsey	Iceland	Born from the sea in 1963.
Vesuvius	Italy	Eruption in 79 A.D. buried Pompeii. Still active, with the most recent eruption in 1944.
Fuji	Japan	A beautiful, snow-capped volcano; last erupted 1707.

© Marvin L. Dembinsky, Jr.

Kinds of Volcanoes

The shape of a volcano is a clue to its history and type. Here are some typical kinds of volcanoes:

• Stratovolcano—This is what people usually think of as the typical volcano. It is built up in layers of the fiery liquid rock known as lava and solid debris blown out of the crater. The beautiful volcanoes Mt. Fujiyama in Japan, and Mt. Hood in Oregon, are stratovolcanoes.

• Cinder cones—These are generally small volcanoes built mainly of solid debris heaped around a vent. Paricutin volcano is a cinder cone.

Volcanic craters build up over many eruptions. The layers of ash and many other materials deposited after each eruption can be seen at the top of the crater in the picture, the Bandera Crater in New Mexico (top). Steam rises from a vent of the Mauna Loa Volcano in Hawaii (bottom). This huge volcano last erupted in 1984. Like its neighbor, Kilauea, Mauna Loa produces huge lava flows.

© J.S. Sroka/Marvin Dembinsky Photo Associates

• Shield volcano—When runny lava flows quietly out of a vent, rather than explosively, it spreads a long way, forming a large, gently sloping volcano. The best example is Mauna Loa on the Big Island of Hawaii, the largest, if not the tallest, volcano in the world.

• Caldera—Sometimes, a volcano ejects so much magma that suddenly the upper slopes of the mountain are unsupported. They collapse inward, creating a huge crater called a caldera. Crater Lake in Oregon is a caldera formed by an enormous eruption 7,000 years ago.

© Marvin L. Dembinsky, Jr.

Crater Lake (top) *fills the crater of the extinct volcano, Mt. Mazama, in Oregon. The lake is about five miles in diameter and nearly 2,000 feet deep.* Mt. Hood (bottom) *in Oregon is a beautiful example of a stratovolcano. It has the classic volcano shape, built by adding layer upon layer of ash, lava, and cinders.*

© Gary Braasch

This "curtain of fire" spurts from a crack in the earth caused by Kilauea Volcano in Hawaii, in July, 1986.

What Comes Out of a Volcano?

Lava is the name for the hot, liquid rock that is known as *magma* when it's underground. As a group, solids ejected by a volcano are called *pyroclastics*. Dust and sand-sized particles are called *ash*; larger particles—up to golf-ball size—are *cinders*; larger particles are *blocks*.

Hot Spots

The Big Island of Hawaii, in the middle of the Pacific Ocean, is made of five volcanoes. One hasn't erupted for sixty thousand years. One has been erupting constantly since 1983. The Hawaiian Islands are the bull's-eye of the Pacific "Ring of Fire."

Yet, by the theory of plate tectonics, there shouldn't be any volcanoes in the middle of the Pacific. Volcanoes, after all, are produced when one plate dives beneath another, only to melt at great depth. The volcanoes of the Hawaiian Islands are far from the edges of the Pacific plate.

There's another riddle about the Hawaiian chain. The islands extend northwest in a nearly straight line more than twelve hundred miles to Midway Island. The Big Island, furthest southeast, is the youngest—less than one million years old, based on dating of its rocks. The islands get steadily older all the way to Midway, which is about twenty-eight million years old. What accounts for the volcanoes being in the middle of the plate and for their age pattern?

The answer that scientists have come up with is called the "Hot Spot" theory. It says that underneath the Pacific plate, where the Big Island is today, is a source of great heat that causes magma to rise to the crust. The heat source, possibly plumes of hot rock rising from deep within the earth, doesn't move. But the Pacific plate above it moves slowly northwest.

The Big Island is directly over the hot spot now, accounting for its volcanoes. As it moves away, its volcanoes will become extinct and new ones will rise to take their place.

The Ring of Fire

On a map of the world, place your finger at the southern tip of South America, Tierra del Fuego ("Land of Fire" in Spanish). Trace the west coast of South America, continue through Central America and the west coast of North America, then swing across the Aleutian Islands and back south to Japan, the Philippines, New Guinea, and finally New Zealand. You have traced almost a complete circle around the Pacific Ocean.

On this circuit are most of the world's six hundred active volcanoes. About 75 percent of the strong earthquakes also strike this region. No wonder seismologists, naturalists, and others refer to it as "The Ring of Fire."

The volcanoes of the Ring are the products of one plate descending beneath another (subduction). When the edge of the diving plate reaches a depth of sixty to one hundred miles, it melts. The magma then flows to the surface.

Several of the island chains in the Pacific are known as island arcs. These islands are pushed up when two plates collide under water. They are marked by many volcanoes. Japan, for example, has about fifty volcanoes.

The "Ring of Fire" extends around the edge of the Pacific Ocean. Volcanoes and earthquakes (triangles) *mark where crustal plates meet.*

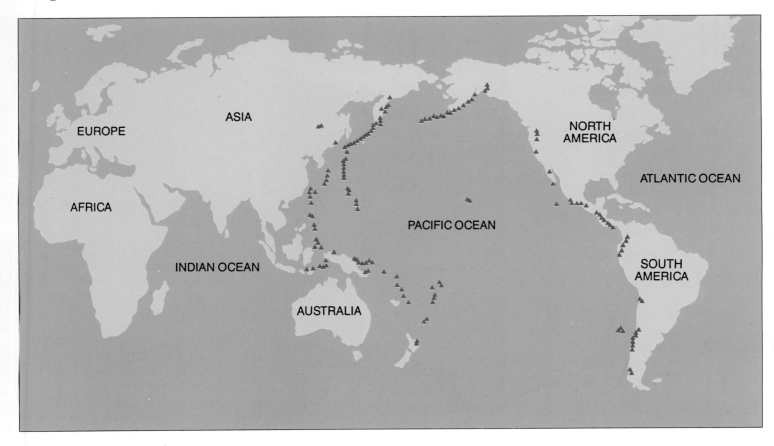

Kilauea

Since Kilauea began erupting on the main island of Hawaii just after New Year's in 1983, the volcano has hardly been still. By 1989, it had poured out 850 million cubic meters of lava, enough to pave a highway circling the earth four times. Since no one is using the lava to pave such a highway, the island of Hawaii is growing a little larger.

As volcanoes go, Kilauea's eruptions are quiet, with lava flowing down its flanks in fiery rivers. The lava exposed to the air cools and hardens. But within the shell, lava remains super-hot and continues to flow. The hardened rock on the outside is such a good insulator that rock on the inside may remain molten for more than ten years.

The lava that flows from Kilauea forms two kinds of rock: aa (pronounced *ahh*), which is rough, and pahoehoe (*pa-hoy-hoy*) which is smooth.

People who live on the flanks of Kilauea will now and then witness a river of lava invading someone's house. More than 60 have been lost since the latest eruption started in 1983 (no person has been killed). When lava destroyed one house in April 1990, a resident of the area told *The New York Times*, "Everybody's nervous, but nobody wants to admit it. People don't freak out here. This is Hawaii. Everybody is taking it slow and easy." Another person said, "It's a party atmosphere." It probably wasn't his house.

A fountain of lava gushes from the growing Puu Oo cone of Kilauea.

WATER

The earth has been called the "Blue Planet." The oceans, seas, gulfs, bays, and other saltwater bodies that give our planet a blue tint when viewed from space make up 71 percent of the earth's surface.

Ninety-seven percent of all the world's water is saltwater found in the oceans of the earth. Only 3 percent is freshwater. And almost all of that freshwater, about 87 percent, is locked up in the ice caps of Antarctica and Greenland and in mountain glaciers. A further 12 percent of freshwater is found underground. This water is vitally important in providing drinking water to people around the world, who draw it up from wells with buckets and pumps. Finally, just 1 percent of the world's freshwater can be found in ponds, lakes, streams, and rivers.

THE OCEANS

In some sense, all the world's oceans are one big global ocean, covering about 142 million square miles. Nevertheless, people usually recognize five oceans—the Pacific, Atlantic, Indian, Southern, and Arctic—and numerous smaller seas.

The largest ocean is the Pacific, covering about sixty-three million square miles. It is shrinking at the rate of a few inches a year. Meanwhile, the Atlantic, the second largest ocean at thirty-two million square miles, is growing by a few inches a year. As you might imagine, there is a connection between the two.

Running down the middle of the Atlantic is the mid-ocean ridge, a submarine mountain range stretching ten thousand miles. It marks the spreading zone of two plates, the North American to the west and the Eurasian to the east. The two plates are pulling apart—called *rifting*—and magma is pushing up to fill in the space. The mid-ocean ridge makes an appearance above ground in the form of the island called Iceland, which is one of the most volcanic places in the world.

As the North American plate moves west and the Eurasian plate moves east, the Pacific Ocean is getting squeezed from both sides. But it shouldn't get noticeably smaller during your lifetime.

The oceans are a powerful and ever-changing force on the earth. They have a huge influence on the weather, spawning hurricanes and cyclones. They keep continents cooler in summer and warmer in winter. The pounding of ocean waves upon the shore releases a great amount of energy, which erodes shorelines and, in some places, is harnessed for electrical power.

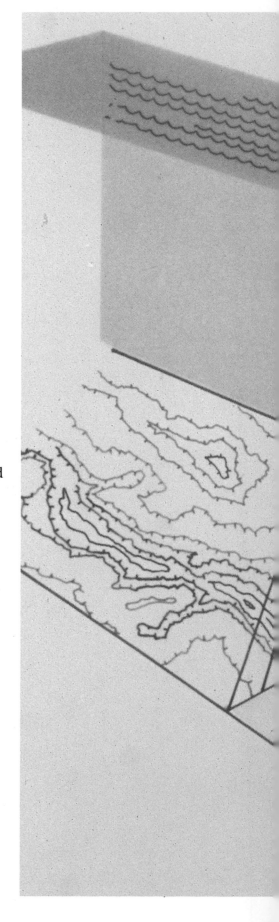

THE WATER CYCLE

Water doesn't stay in one place very long. One exception, of course, is when water is ice. In this solid form, molecules of water can remain in the same place for hundreds of thousands, even millions, of years.

The average molecules of H_2O in the middle of the ocean aren't as static as ice. They may get gulped by a fish. Or they may evaporate from the surface of the ocean, turning into water vapor. The winds above the ocean will blow these gaseous molecules of water around. If the conditions are right, the vapor may turn back into liquid form, making many drops of water molecules. More than likely, these water molecules will land back in the ocean. But sometimes they will fall as rain, snow, or some other form of precipitation on land. What then?

They may sink into the ground. There, they might be taken in by the roots of a plant. Or they might travel down until they reach a great underwater ocean called groundwater. Groundwater moves, sometimes very slowly. The water molecules might travel for years. They might flow into someone's well, where people can drink them. They might flow into a lake. Or they might end up in a small stream. The stream might carry them to a small river, which might take them to a larger river, which—if these molecules haven't gotten lost along the way—might transport them all the way back to the ocean.

Once they reach the ocean, the molecules start to move through the water cycle all over again. This constant motion of water through the cycle is the way in which water cleanses and purifies itself.

Underwater Mountains

About 50 percent of the Pacific floor and somewhat less of the Atlantic is made up of the *abyssal plain,* a relatively flat part of the ocean floor that is deeper than two miles in most places. But, the bottom of an ocean is not all flat. It has mountains and canyons, just like a continent.

A mountain range called the mid-ocean ridge snakes through all the oceans, making it the longest mountain range on earth. Many of its peaks are taller than 10,000 feet, and stick above the ocean as islands. The tallest mountain in the world, in fact, may be Mauna Kea, on the island of Hawaii, which rises nearly 14,000 feet above sea level, but measures more than thirty-two thousand feet from the Pacific Ocean floor.

Underwater Valleys

The Pacific Ocean has the deepest valleys and canyons on the earth. Where an oceanic plate meets another plate, it dives down into the *mantle,* the layer of the earth underneath the crust. This creates a trench. A map of the Pacific shows trenches all around the Ring of Fire, where one plate dives beneath another. The world's deepest trench lies just east of the Marianas Islands in the western Pacific. It reaches a depth of 36,198 feet, or almost seven miles.

A research ship from the Scripps Institution of Oceanography in San Diego maps the ocean floor. It uses an instrument called Sea Beam, a sonar system which bounces sound waves off the ocean floor. A computer "reads" the echoes to generate the map.

Courtesy Scripps Institution of Oceanography/University of California, San Diego

TSUNAMI

It was morning on the 27th of August, 1883. An uninhabited island named Krakatoa, located in the Sunda strait of Indonesia, had just been completely destroyed by the volcano that was its core. That volcano had been erupting since May, sending dust and steam into the air. But after several days of rumbling in August, the island erupted three times beginning in the small hours of the night. The biggest of the explosions was heard in Perth, Australia—1,902 miles away.

Krakatoa is often remembered as the volcano that obliterated itself, or as the volcano that put so much ash into the air that sunsets around the world were affected for two years afterward. But it is also the volcano that created huge waves that swamped the villages on the neighboring islands of Java and Sumatra, killing 36,000 people. These kinds of waves are called *tsunami,* which is Japanese for "harbor waves." Some people call them tidal waves, but they have absolutely nothing to do with tides.

A Japanese print by Hokusai, called "The Wave." Notice how the wave appears to dwarf Mt. Fujiyama in the distance.

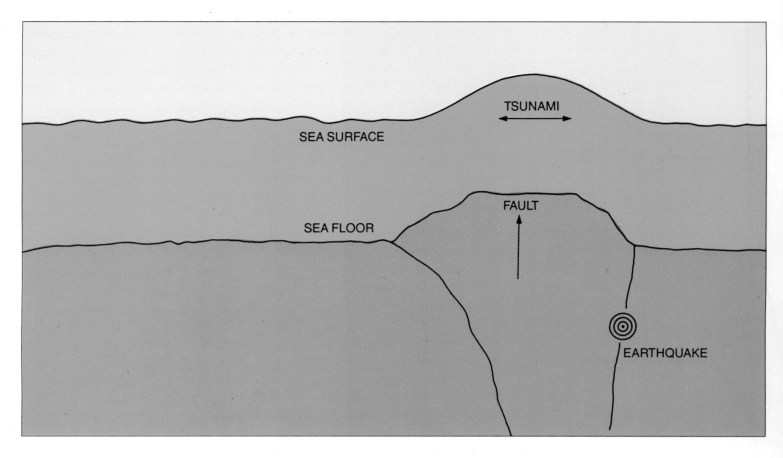

Labels on diagram: TSUNAMI, SEA SURFACE, SEA FLOOR, FAULT, EARTHQUAKE

A tsunami may occur when a block of the ocean's crust is thrust upward or downward along a fault. The movement of the ocean's floor disturbs the ocean's surface, causing a bulge. The bulge travels as a tsunami, possibly for great distances. Tsunamis and earthquakes often go hand in hand.

Earthquakes Under The Ocean

In his book, *Darkest Hours*, Jay Robert Nash quotes a man who was aboard a ship not too far from Krakatoa when it blew:

"Suddenly, we saw a gigantic wave ...advancing from the seashore with considerable speed....Before our eyes this terrifying upheaval of the sea, in a sweeping transit, consumed in one instant the ruin of the town; the lighthouse fell in one piece, and all the houses of the town were swept away in one blow like a castle of cards."

Tsunamis are usually caused by undersea earthquakes. When the crust at a fault moves up or down, the surface of the sea mimics the change. If the fault slips, the water at the surface dips; if the fault thrusts up, the surface will form a dome. This unevenness can't last, but it puts in motion a tsunami.

A Wall of Water

On the open sea, the tsunami may not be noticeable. It may be only a few feet high. And it travels four hundred miles-per-hour or faster in deep water. But as it comes into shallow water, it slows down. The faster moving water behind the wave can then pile up, until the wall of water may be thirty feet or more in height.

It's hard to put a tape measure to a tsunami, but one in Alaska's Prince William Sound after the earthquake there in 1964 is thought to have exceeded two hundred feet.

A tsunami can travel across an entire ocean. So when an earthquake struck off southern Chile in 1960, a tsunami hit the Hawaiian Islands fifteen hours later, leaving sixty one dead and 282 injured. Nine hours after that, part of the same wave hit Japan. Boats were tossed inland. Ports were destroyed. Five thousand houses were wiped out. In all 180 people died and fifty thousand were left homeless.

In Hot Water

In Wyoming's Yellowstone National Park, the geyser called Old Faithful shoots boiling water one hundred feet and more into the air every hour, give or take twenty minutes.

In Iceland, most people have hot water that's been heated naturally in the ground, not by a hot-water heater in their basements.

Just below the surface of the ground in these two places are large bodies of magma—molten rock. As water trickles down from the surface, it is heated by the hot rock and travels back to the surface. The water may be used directly, as it is in Iceland. Or, if the water is hot enough, the steam may be used to generate electricity. This is called geothermal energy—the power of the volcano. Some places that tap geothermal energy include California, Hawaii, Iceland, New Zealand, and Italy.

LAKES

Three of the biggest lakes in the world show the different ways that lakes can form.

The largest inland body of water in the world is the Caspian Sea, which, at 143,244 square miles, is about the size of Montana. The salty Caspian, located between Iran and the Soviet Union, is thought to have once been connected to the world's oceans, but later became isolated by plate movements.

The largest freshwater lake, in surface area, is Lake Superior, one of the Great Lakes of the United States. It is the size of South Carolina. Lake Superior and the other Great Lakes were formed by the glaciers, the great tongues of ice that covered the northern part of North America until 10,000 years ago. When the glaciers became smaller as the climate warmed, large chunks of ice remained behind in basins. Eventually, the ice melted and the basins became the Great Lakes.

Another way a lake can form is when the crust stretches apart on either side of a fault. Or in an area with many faults, one block of crust may drop, relative to the ones around it. Some of the world's most interesting lakes formed from such earth movements.

One such lake is Lake Baikal, in the Soviet Union. It is only the eighth largest lake in area, but it is by far the deepest lake in the world, reaching down more than one mile in places. Lake Baikal holds so much water that the water of all the Great Lakes would fit in it. In fact, roughly one-fifth of all the fresh-water in the world is contained in Lake Baikal.

Lake Superior, between the United States and Canada, is the largest body of fresh water in the world, covering more than 30,000 square miles. The lake is used for transportation, for food, and for recreation. This scene is from Lake Superior Provincial Park on the Canadian side of the lake.

Salt Lakes

The Dead Sea is one of the world's great salt lakes, where the water is much saltier than ocean water. In addition, it is the lowest point on the earth's surface, some 1,302 feet below sea level.

If a lake has no outlet, no drain to the sea, it will become salty. Rivers and streams bring minerals into the lake; evaporation removes water, leaving behind a lake that is more dense with salt and minerals. The Dead Sea between Israel and Jordan is the world's most concentrated body of water. It is ten times more salty than any ocean. Swimmers find it very difficult to dive beneath the surface since the salt water makes them so buoyant.

Utah's Great Salt Lake is almost as salty as the Dead Sea. The lake expands and contracts depending on the amount of runoff it receives from the nearby mountains, so that it becomes more or less salty, depending on the weather.

Caves

Caves are usually made by the action of groundwater. As an underground stream flows it becomes naturally acidic in places. When the slightly acidic water meets soft rock called limestone, it eats the rock away.

This erosion doesn't take place very quickly. It may take 10,000 years for a small crack in the limestone to grow to the width of a pencil. Over millions of years, a cave system the size of Mammoth Cave in Kentucky can result. Mammoth has at least 300 miles of caves.

Hanging from the ceilings of many caves are large icicle-like structures called stalactites. As drops of water fall from the ceiling, they hang briefly, depositing some calcium carbonate. Gradually, the calcium carbonate builds up into a stalactite.

Where the drops fall on the floor of the cave, they may deposit more calcium carbonate. At that place, a stalagmite grows up, like a reverse icicle, to meet the stalactite.

RIVERS

What the earth builds, it also destroys. No feature on the face of the planet is permanent. So, while the collision of plate upon plate pushes up great mountain ranges, the force of moving water helps to bring them down.

A young river typically comes out of a steep mountain and falls fast and straight. The power of the water, mixed with pieces of rock, rapidly cuts a steep-sided valley. If the river flows over both hard and soft rock, it may erode the soft rock faster, forming a waterfall.

The beginning of a river is called its source. The source may be a lake, a spring, or a glacier. A river valley that has had a glacier in it looks different from one that has never been glaciated. A glaciated valley typically is U-shaped (meaning the river is at the bottom of the U and the hills or mountains form the sides of the U). Ice moving through a valley acts like a giant earth-mover, scraping away rocks and soil and piling them up at one end of the valley. A valley that has never been glaciated will be V-shaped, with much steeper sides.

As a river ages, it erodes its bed, gradually becoming flatter and slower. The sign of an older river is a flat valley, within which the river has begun to meander. Meander is a technical term for a river that turns this way and that like a snake.

The world's longest river, the Nile, flows quietly near the

Aswan Dam in Egypt, on the way to its mouth at the

Mediterranean Sea.

60   WATER

Angel Falls

The world's tallest waterfall is Angel Falls, in Venezuela. Water going over the falls drops a total of 3,212 feet—more than half a mile, or two times around an Olympic track. Also impressive are the Khone Falls on the Mekong River in southern Laos. They're only 70 feet high, but more water passes over them every second than over any other waterfall in the world. One second's worth of water from that waterfall would fill more than 100 backyard swimming pools. With all waterfalls, as the force of the river gradually cuts down through the rock, the incline gradually levels out.

Older and Longer Rivers

The world's longest rivers are all reasonably mature rivers. They are broad and flat, with gentle mean-

ders. They carry large amounts of sediment. Some of the load of dirt gets dropped along the river banks to form broad floodplains. Some gets deposited where the river meets the sea, creating a fan shaped delta.

The Nile in Africa is the longest, flowing 4,187 miles from its source. The Amazon of South America is the next longest, at 3,915 miles. The Amazon begins as a trickle high on the eastern side of the Andes Mountains, in Peru, and very quickly becomes a large river. Most of the river runs very slowly, and it is so wide—four to six miles in places—that sometimes you can't see all the way across it. More than half the rivers of South America drain into the Amazon. Many of these tributaries are mighty rivers in their own right, including four that are more than one thousand miles long: the Purus (2,100 miles), the Madeira (2,031 miles), the Japura (1,750 miles), and the Negro (1,400 miles).

Here, the Amazon River meanders through Peru, thousands of miles from its mouth in the Atlantic Ocean of northeastern Brazil. At 3,915 miles in length, it is second only to the Nile River in Africa. Angel Falls, in Venezuela (opposite page), *is the world's tallest waterfall, at more than 3,200 feet. Waterfalls form when rushing water flows over erosion resistant rock and cuts down through softer rock.*

Grand Canyon

The cutting power of water is nowhere better shown than in the Grand Canyon. Beginning 10 million years or so ago, the Colorado River cut down through the Colorado Plateau. The result is the world's biggest river gorge, one mile deep, twelve miles wide in places, and 200 miles long. Major John Wesley Powell, who led the exploration of the Canyon in the middle 1800s, wrote, "The wonders of the Grand Canyon cannot be adequately represented in symbols of speech, nor by speech itself."

The Grand Canyon was formed over millions of years by the cutting power of the Colorado River. Located largely in northeast Arizona, the canyon is as much as 18 miles wide and one mile deep. On the next page are Lower Falls, which cut through Yellowstone National Park.

FLOODS

A flood is too much water where humans don't want it. But floods are a natural part of the way the world works. Rivers will always overflow their banks; high tides and high winds will combine to push the ocean up over coastal areas.

People are attracted to river areas that are prone to floods because floods deposit silt along the banks of the river, making the soil richer. Every few years, a huge surge of water will come down the river, as a result of too much rain, or too much snow melting upstream, and the river will pour over its banks. The resulting flood may ruin crops, flush people out of their homes, and even kill them. But the silt replaces nutrients that have been removed from the soil by years of intensive farming. So after the flood waters are gone, farmers return to rebuild their homes and replant their crops.

The largely flat country of Bangladesh is nestled below the Himalayas to the north and the Bay of Bengal to the south. Floods are a common occurrence, as storms bring waters from the bay, or the rivers overflow with runoff from the eroded lower slopes of the Himalayas. Citizens of the capital, Dacca, move around their city in boats, rafts, and even a bicycle rickshaw.

DEADLY FLOODS

Yellow River, China 1931	3,700,000 dead
Yellow River, 1887	900,000 dead
Conemaugh River, Johnstown, Pennsylvania, May 31, 1889	2,200 dead
Lake Okeechobee, Florida, Sept. 13, 1928	2,000 dead

How Trees Prevent Floods

On the southern slopes of the Himalayas, where India and Nepal meet, the forests are disappearing. The rapidly growing populations in the area are cutting the trees for building materials and for firewood. In most of the world's poorer countries wood is the main fuel for cooking and heating.

The result of this widespread deforestation is that floods are getting worse in the river valleys below the mountains. Why should cutting a tree on a mountain slope increase the chance of a flood a few hundred miles downstream?

When rainwater lands on a slope, its eventual destination is the ocean. But it might be waylaid by trees and other vegetation that act as sponges. Their roots absorb some water. And they hold the soil in place, which further slows the runoff of water.

Without trees, the heavy rains that hit during monsoon season erode the slopes. The water isn't delayed in its path to the sea. So rivers fill up much more rapidly, and overflow their banks.

Erosion takes place all over the world. As a country grows more prosperous, farmland is paved over with asphalt and concrete for highways, malls, and new suburbs. Water doesn't sink into asphalt the way it does into soil. The result is that when it rains, the water runs off more rapidly into streams, raising their levels.

Tree seedlings grown in this greenhouse in Quebec are used for reforestation (top). Planting trees in deforested areas (bottom) helps prevent erosion and flooding.

© Harold V. Green/Valan Photos

The Mississippi River, as seen near Hannibal, Missouri (above), eventually captures water that falls as rain or snow on nearly half the surface of the continental United States. In its upper reaches, the river is slow-moving and meandering—typical of an older river. But south of Minneapolis, people have tried to manage the river (below, and opposite page) to improve transportation and agriculture. The river doesn't always behave as planned.

Taming the Mississippi

The Mississippi River is very broad and sluggish in places. But as its waters rise toward flood stage, it can become a raging and unpredictable force. When a small river runs out of control, it's a problem. When the Mississippi runs out of control, it's a disaster.

The Mississippi, after all, is the mightiest river in North America. Rainwater and meltwater from 1,246,000 square miles—fully 41 percent of the entire continental United States—eventually finds its way into the Mississippi. What does the Corps of Engineers use to try to tame the river?

Levees As in China and elsewhere around the world, mankind builds earthen walls to try to prevent high water from spilling out into the surrounding lowlands. More than 2,200 miles of levees help confine the waters of the Mississippi.

Floodways At several places along the lower Mississippi, there are almost empty channels ready to take overflow from the Mississippi. These floodways carry high water around towns, preventing flooding there.

Channelization The Corps dredges the river channel to make it deeper for navigation and also to improve its ability to carry water. It puts dikes out into the water to make the river flow swiftly down the center of the channel. This keeps the channel deep and less likely to overflow.

Dams The Corps has built more than twenty dams on the Mississippi itself and many on its tributaries to help control the flow of water. Dams create reservoirs behind them, which can hold excess water during times of heavy runoff.

© Design Photography

China's Sorrow

The Yellow River of China has many distinctions:

It is one of the world's longest, at about 2,900 miles. It is perhaps the world's siltiest river, meaning that it carries more fine particles of rock and soil than any other river. If 3 percent of the total weight of a river's flow is sediment (and 97 percent is water), that's considered high. Along parts of its length, the Yellow is up to 46 percent silt.

Finally, the Yellow is a killer. During its regular floods, it has killed millions of Chinese.

The Yellow River's source is in the mountains of Tibet, in western China. It flows north toward Mongolia, makes a wide turn to the south and eventually flows out to the sea. It flows through lands that have been deforested for a thousand years, carrying a billion tons of silt a year out of the mountains and hills. The color of the silt gives the river its name.

After it leaves a plateau region, it runs through a large flat floodplain. The Yellow River built that flood plain. Whenever a river overflows its

banks, it immediately slows down. The sediment suspended in the swift-flowing water then settles out. Some of the sediment is deposited on the bed of the river itself, raising it up. Some is deposited just beyond the river banks, creating fertile farm land.

Over the years, the Chinese have tried to defend themselves from the river by building levees. These are simply earthen walls built on the river banks to contain the water when it rises. Unfortunately, levees break, leading to floods and the deposit of sediment just described.

When the Chinese repair the levees, they also make them higher. They have to because the silt deposited during floods has caused the river bottom to be raised *above* the surrounding flood plain. Picture a river that in places is fifteen feet *above* the surrounding plain, kept in line only by the walls that surround it. When a levee does break, water can flow through it and spread out for thousands of square miles.

Perhaps the greatest flood on the Yellow came in 1887. Heavy rains combined with poorly maintained levees to cause a half-mile break in the dike. As a result, a town ten miles away from the river was soon situated on the bottom of a new lake the size of Lake Ontario. In all, more than two thousand villages and towns were swamped. People who didn't drown died of the cold as they had no shelter. Others who survived the cold (the flood started in September) perished from famine. The flood waters destroyed crops that were ready to be harvested. More than one million people died from this one flood.

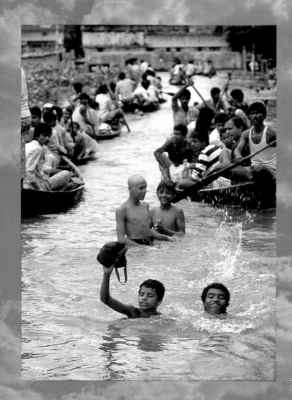

AIR

This book treats the earth in three parts: the land itself, the waters on the land, and the air that surrounds the planet. Of the three parts, the air is perhaps the most mysterious. It is largely invisible, but it has a great effect on everything humans do.

Without air, there wouldn't be life on earth. But at the same time, problems associated with the air cause a lot of problems for the planet. Hurricanes, tornadoes and other killer storms roar through the air, whipping up dust and debris and destroying houses, boats, and trees. Dry air devastates large areas of continents, causing droughts and deserts. And air pollution caused by humans warms the world by fouling the atmosphere and keeping heat from radiating away into space.

HURRICANES, CYCLONES, TYPHOONS, WILLY-WILLIES

The most fearsome storms in the world go by many different names, depending on where they occur. In the tropical Atlantic Ocean, they're called hurricanes. In the Pacific, they're known as typhoons, except for some places in Australia, where they are called willy-willies. And in the Indian Ocean they are cyclones.

These storms are born in the warm oceans just north and south of the equator. Warm air, full of water vapor from the ocean, rises. As it rises, more warm moist air rushes in from below to take its place. A thunderstorm brews because the water vapor in the rising currents of air *condenses*. That means that water vapor, a gas, changes to liquid water droplets. Condensation releases heat, which fuels the growing storm by keeping air currents rising.

A typical hurricane starts as a low-pressure system near the African coast and moves westward with the prevailing winds. Somehow—scientists don't completely understand how—the rising winds in a storm begin to spin (counterclockwise in the Northern Hemisphere, clockwise in the Southern). As the spinning winds increase in speed, the tropical low-pressure system becomes a hurricane.

Palm trees are blown by a fierce tropical storm.

KILLER STORMS

Cyclone	November, 1970	Bangladesh	300,000 dead
Cyclone	October, 1942	India	40,000 dead
Cyclone	May, 1985	Bangladesh	10,000 dead
Typhoon	September, 1984	Philippines	1,363 dead
Tornadoes	March, 1925	United States	689 dead
Tornadoes	April, 1974	United States	350 dead

Because the pressure is lowest in the center of the storm, called the eye, the winds spiral in toward the eye from the edge of the hurricane. The warm ocean is essential, because it provides the water vapor that feeds energy to the hurricane. That heat energy, from condensation, drives the rapid air movement in the hurricane.

Hurricanes can be extremely large storms, 100 miles to more than 500 miles across. As they approach land, they push the seas in front of them, often causing coastal floods. It is often said that rising seas are the result of the extremely low air pressure at the center of the hurricane, which isn't able to "force" the sea down. But Miles Laurence, a hurricane specialist at the National Hurricane Center in Florida, says that the main reason for the rising seas is the high wind of the hurricane pushing the water ahead of it.

The storm surge of high water and the high winds are responsible for most of the destruction in a hurricane.

When a hurricane hits land, or when it wanders north over the ocean, its intensity drops. Why? Hurricane scientist Laurence says that without moisture from warm water, the hurricane just runs out of gas.

Seas rise in front of the strong winds of a hurricane, surging

forward to damage coastal property and toss yachts about.

Hurricane Gilbert lashed the

Caribbean in September, 1988 (right).

In Jamaica, winds blew down trees and

buildings and upended this plane

(below). Notice the sign in the

foreground. The hurricane weakened

somewhat before it hit the coast near

the border of Texas and Mexico.

Hurricane Gilbert

In the middle of September 1988, a hurricane named Gilbert swooped out of the eastern Atlantic to lash Jamaica and Mexico's Yucatan Peninsula. It has been called the worst hurricane of the century, and its statistics bear that name out:

- 185 mile-per-hour winds with gusts of over 200 miles-per-hour
- $10 billion in damage
- 400 dead

For meteorologists, probably the most important measure of a hurricane's strength is the air pressure at its center. Gilbert's air pressure was measured at 26.13, the lowest ever recorded. Air pressure rises and falls daily, but ordinarily it stays within the range 29-31.

Two other numbers that describe Gilbert are seemingly contradictory. The total width of the storm was enormous, 500 miles across. Yet its eye was smaller than usual, only eight miles across instead of the typical twenty five. Frederick Gadonski, a meteorologist from Pennsylvania State University, explained why such a small eye was so lethal, in an interview in *The New York Times* as Gilbert lashed Jamaica: "Its concentrated winds are cutting a tornado-like path of destruction. But unlike a tornado's swath, which is only a few hundred yards wide, this hurricane's path of devastation is some fifty miles wide."

In other words, the winds surrounding Gilbert's smaller eye were much more powerful than the winds surrounding the larger eye of most hurricanes. Even though the eye itself was only eight miles wide, the strong winds around it spread out for tens of miles.

Into the Eye of the Hurricane

Hurricane hunting. The job sounds romantic, but it means flying into a storm in search of the calm at the eye of the hurricane. The National Oceanic and Atmospheric Administration (NOAA), the parent of the weather service, began sending weather scientists into hurricanes in 1960. NOAA uses four-engine propeller planes, each carrying about $7 million worth of high-tech gear.

Guided by radar that shows wind speed and direction, the planes make a harrowing ride to the eye. The eye is surrounded by a thick wall of clouds—the eyewall. In the eye, winds drop to almost zero. With the buffeting temporarily halted, the crew and scientists have a spectacular sight: towering clouds all around and, sometimes, sunny skies above.

Soon, though, the plane plunges back through the eyewall and into the region around it, which has the most intense winds of the storm.

Hurricane Gilbert shows up clearly on this weather map. The eye of the hurricane, the clear spot in the center of the swirling clouds, is located just south of Brownsville, Texas, about to hit the coast.

Following a 1988 cyclone in Bangladesh, some people make their way along city streets in boats; others wade or swim.

The Killer Cyclone

Bangladesh is one of the poorest countries in the world. Located just east of India, it was once part of Pakistan, called East Pakistan. It is about the size of Wisconsin, but it has a population of 110 million people, equal to 40 percent of the population of the United States.

Bangladesh is a country formed by rivers. Two great rivers, the Ganges and the Brahmaputra, enter the Bay of Bengal after a meandering journey through the country. There, the rivers deposit a huge amount of silt to make the largest river delta in the world. The islands of the delta are heavily populated, because the flood plain soil is extremely fertile.

Bangladesh sits at the top of the Bay of Bengal, which occasionally acts like a funnel and directs cyclones toward the low coast of the country. Only a low sea wall protects the people from the sea.

In October 1970, a cyclone hit the coast. People had been warned by Radio Pakistan to expect a big storm, but the damage turned out to be less than expected. A month later, the radio again issued cyclone warnings, but these were partly ignored because the earlier cyclone hadn't been as bad as expected. And in truth, there wasn't much the peasant farmers could do. They couldn't escape into the interior easily, because there were few roads or rail lines. They couldn't travel up the rivers, which were near flood stage. And they couldn't abandon their livestock.

On the night of November 12, the cyclone struck, pushing a 50-foot wall of water in front of it. Since most of the islands of the delta are fewer than 20 feet above sea level, they were all swamped. After the wave broke, it washed back out to sea, carrying people, livestock, and debris with it.

Communications with other parts of the country, never good to begin with, were dead. The capital, Dacca, didn't learn the full details of the disaster for two days.

For survivors, the worst was still ahead. Most had no clean fresh-water supply, and so had to drink polluted water. There was no dry ground in which to bury the bodies. The crops, which were just about to be harvested, were wiped out; many people later died of starvation.

Since 1970, Bangladesh has been hit by other cyclones. In 1988, three-quarters of the country was flooded and 30 million people were left homeless. The president's residence in Dacca was knee deep in water.

The spiral nature of cyclones is seen clearly in this shot of one near Hawaii, taken from above the clouds. The center of the cyclone is a region of low pressure. The winds spiral around toward the center. A cyclone in the Atlantic Ocean is called a hurricane.

Terrifying Twister

With wind speeds of 300 mph and more, tornadoes are nature's most violent storms. They are so destructive that myths have developed about them. For example, it is widely believed that the low air pressure inside a tornado can cause a building to explode outward. Tornadoes can reduce a building to rubble, but as a result of high winds, not a drop in pressure.

Tornadoes develop out of violent thunderstorms, where hot, humid air meets a cold front. Often, heavy hail accompanies a tornado and the funnel cloud becomes dark and visible as it sucks up dirt and debris. This flying debris is the main cause of injuries and deaths.

Such conditions are common in the Great Plains states and the southeastern U.S., especially in April, May, and June. One area that is often struck by the storms, called Tornado Alley, stretches from the Texas panhandle through Oklahoma and Kansas, into Missouri, Illinois, and Indiana.

This tornado struck Osnabrook, North Dakota, on July 24, 1978. The thin, gray funnel cloud stretches to the ground from the turbulent layer of clouds above.

Some Tornado Facts

• *One sign of a tornado is the sound it makes, which has been described as similar to the roar of a nearby airplane.*

• *Tornado wind speeds increase with the height of the tornado.*

• *The safest places to be during a tornado are in specially designed storm cellars. Lacking a storm cellar, other safe places include against the wall in a sturdily built basement, or in a small interior room of a house, such as a bathroom or closet.*

• *Trying to outrun a tornado is usually not a wise idea. They can travel up to 70 miles-per-hour, though 30 miles-per-hour is more common.*

DROUGHT

"Not as much water as the people need."

This quote from a minister of agriculture in the African nation of Niger, is about as good a definition of drought as one can give. Floods are probably the most common natural disaster. Earthquakes and cyclones are the most deadly. But droughts, though not nearly so dramatic, probably affect more people than any other natural disaster.

Droughts are not just about rainfall, or lack of it. Strictly speaking, there is no drought in the Sahara Desert. Though there's no rainfall, no one expects any so the people of the desert experience no additional hardship. They've learned to do without. But when expected moisture fails to come, or does not last when it comes, the result is a drought.

One of the worst droughts in the world this century took place between 1968 and 1973 in a region of western Africa just south of the Sahara called the Sahel. The region's rain tends to fall in only a few months of the year. Farmers are able to grow some crops, but traditionally the people have been nomadic, following the rains with their herds of cattle.

The Sahara Desert is one of the driest places on the planet,

with some parts receiving no rain for years. In the desert you

don't expect rain. But when parts of the globe that normally

receive adequate rain don't get any, the resulting drought can

be a human disaster. Drought is one of the most wide-spread of

human disasters.

AIR 87

As countries became independent in the area, the nomadic people began to settle in one place. Governments dug wells so that water would be available all year round. When the rate of rainfall diminished in the late 1960s, conditions were ripe for disaster.

As nomads, the people would have searched farther for water. But in settlements, they used wells heavily until they were depleted. Cattle which ordinarily would be allowed to wander in search of water trampled the ground around the wells. Grasses gave way to sand. People also cut vegetation for firewood and during a drought the vegetation could not recover.

So the drought, which was hard enough on the people, allowed the desert to creep closer. As vegetation disappeared and soils became compacted with the constant trampling, the habitat's ability to store water decreased. That may have made a future drought even more likely.

More than 100,000 people died during the drought in the Sahel from 1968 to 1973. Another drought hit the area during the 1980s. More droughts seem likely in the future.

The Sahel region of Africa, just south of the Sahara, has been experiencing severe drought for the past two decades. Here, cattle and herders walk through the dust in Cameroon. By trampling plants and leaving barren ground, large herds of cattle help make a drought worse.

Antarctica: The unexpected desert

When asked to name the world's greatest desert, most people answer, "Sahara." Few would think of Antarctica, the icy continent surrounding the South Pole, as a desert. But, in fact, Antarctica rivals the Sahara as the world's greatest desert.

Some places in the icy continent's interior, such as at the South Pole, may have less precipitation than the Sahara in a given year. It's simply too cold to snow.

Antarctica is about one-and-a-half times the size of the Sahara. The coastal areas receive much more rain and snow, but the high, central ice cap is every bit as dry as the famous sandy desert.

Of course, the Antarctic is not actually without water. Eight out of every 10 gallons of fresh water found on earth are stored there. It's just that it's frozen. Scientists who work on the frozen continent must collect snow from a "mine" and melt it to get water.

The Antarctic is the coldest region on earth, with temperatures in the interior sometimes dropping to 100 degrees below zero. The continent is also one of the world's driest regions—it is usually too cold to snow.

Going to Extremes

Some of the most extreme weather records are:

• Sunniest: The eastern Sahara Desert of North Africa hardly ever sees a cloud. In an average year, it's sunny 97 percent of daylight hours.

• Hottest: Not surprisingly, the hottest temperature ever recorded is also in the Sahara Desert, at a place in Libya called Al'azizyah. The thermometer registered 136.4°F there on September 13, 1922. In North America, Death Valley, California, has the distinction of recording the hottest temperature: 134°F on July 10, 1913.

• Coldest: The Soviet research station Vostok, which is in the center of the Antarctic continent, has recorded the coldest temperature ever: –126.9°F. The average annual temperature there is –72°F.

• Rainiest: A spot on the Hawaiian island of Kauai has the distinction of being the wettest place on the planet that is not already under water. On the side of Mount Wai-'ale-'ale, which is 5,148 feet above sea level, rain falls about 335 days a year, sometimes as many as 350. The average annual rainfall is an astounding 451 inches. Amazingly, only a few miles away on the same island, the average rainfall is only 20 inches a year.

THE AMAZING EARTH

As you've seen in the preceding pages, the earth is full of amazing sights. Many of these geological features—mountains, canyons, rivers, and lakes—developed over thousands or even millions of years. Many geological processes work much too slowly for us to notice. But with enough time, they can work wonders. For example, millions of years ago, the Atlantic Ocean looked like the Red Sea in the Middle East looks today—long and narrow. And now the Red Sea is slowly growing to look more and more like today's Atlantic Ocean. The land at the opposite shores of the Red Sea, Africa on the west and Saudi Arabia on the east, are moving away from each other at the rate of several inches a year. One hundred million years from now, the Red Sea will be about as wide as the Atlantic is today.

Geology doesn't always work slowly, however. When great forces are unleashed within the earth, on the oceans, or in the atmosphere, natural disasters can result. By understanding the forces of the earth, people can sometimes keep disasters from becoming tragedies. For example, scientists and engineers who study earthquakes know how to make buildings that won't topple in a quake. They can't prevent earthquakes, but they can save many lives.

As much as scientists know about the earth, they're constantly learning more. There are many wonders still to be discovered.

Tanzania, site of this beautiful lake, is part of the East African rift system. Rift valleys are getting wider as the two sides pull apart from each other. The Atlantic Ocean formed from a similar geological process.

METRIC CONVERSIONS

U.S. Units	Metric Equivalents
LINEAR MEASURE	
1 inch	2.54 centimeters
1 foot	0.3048 meters
1 yard	0.9144 meters
1 rod	5.0292 meters
1 mile	1,609.3 meters
1 furlong	201.168 meters
1 league	4.828 kilometers
AREA MEASURE	
1 square inch	6.4516 square centimeters
1 square foot	929.03 square centimeters
1 square yard	0.836 square meters
1 square rod	25.293 square meters
1 acre	0.405 hectares
1 square mile	2.5899 square kilometers
CUBIC MEASURE	
1 cubic inch	16.387 cubic centimeters
1 cubic foot	28.316 cubic centimeters
1 cubic yard	0.765 cubic meters
WEIGHT	
1 ounce	28.350 grams
1 pound	453.592 grams
100 pounds	45.3592 kilograms
1 ton	0.90718 metric tons

Temperature Conversions

°F	°C	°F	°C
32	0	125	51.7
38	3.3	130	54.4
42	5.6	135	57.2
46.4	8	140	60
50	10	145	62.8
55	12.8	150	65.6
60	15.6	155	68.3
65	18.3	160	71.1
70	21.1	165	73.9
75	23.9	170	76.7
80	26.7	175	79.4
85	29.4	180	82.2
90	32.2	185	85
95	35	190	87.8
100	37.8	195	90.6
105	40.6	200	93.3
110	43.3	205	96.1
115	46.1	210	98.9
120	48.9	212	100

To convert Fahrenheit degrees into Centigrade, subtract 32, multiply by 5 and divide by 9. To convert Centigrade into Fahrenheit, multiply by 9, divide by 5 and add 32.

For further reading:

Aylesworth, T. and V. Aylesworth, 1983, *The Mount St. Helens Disaster* (New York: Franklin Watts)

Bolt, Bruce, 1988, *Earthquakes* (New York: W.H. Freeman)*

Branwell, M., 1986, *Volcanoes and Earthquakes* (New York: Franklin Watts)

Decker, Robert and Barbara Decker, 1989, *Volcanoes* (New York: W.H. Freeman)*

Harrington, John, *Dance of the Continents: Adventures with Rocks and Time* (Los Angeles: J.P. Tarcher)*

Kiefer, I., 1978, *Global Jigsaw Puzzle: Story of Continental Drift* (New York: Atheneum)

McPhee, John, 1989, *The Control of Nature* (New York: Farar Straus Giroux)*

Nash, Jay Robert, 1976, *Darkest Hours: A narrative encyclopedia of worldwide disasters from ancient times to the present* (Chicago: Nelson-Hall)

Ritchie, David, 1981, *The Ring of Fire* (New York: Atheneum)*

* = adult book

INDEX